SOULFUL CONNECTIONS:
POETRY OF LOVE, SUPPORT & INSPIRATION
NURTURING BONDS, INSPIRING SOULS

BITUMANI BORAH

INDIA • SINGAPORE • MALAYSIA

ISBN 979-8-89026-928-7

Contents

Chapter 1: Introduction: A Journey of Rediscovery and Inner Strength 5

Chapter 2: Embracing Motherhood: A Journey of Resilience, Support, and Empowerment... 12

Chapter 3: The Soulmate 19

Chapter 4: Weights and Strength! The Power of True Love/Greatest Love 26

Chapter 5: Overcoming Challenges: Showing Up Even at the Lowest Times................... 45

Chapter 6: The Conclusion: Unfolding Life's Canvas .. 85

Chapter 1: Introduction: A Journey of Rediscovery and Inner Strength

In January 2023, I found myself weighed down, both physically and emotionally, tipping the scales at a daunting 100 kilograms. Life seemed like an impossible mountain to climb, until my best friend stepped in, as always – my lifeline, my rock, my guiding light.

With their genuine care and deep concern, something incredible started happening. I've managed to shed twenty-five kilos on my ongoing weight loss journey. But it's not just about the numbers; it's about finding my true self and healing the wounds from the past.

Through the power of divine love and genuine concern, I discovered that anything is possible. The support I received ignited a hidden strength within me, which I was completely unaware of, breaking the chains that held me back since I remember. I realized that when people truly love and care for you, they can help you become a better version of yourself.

As I continue on this journey of self-discovery, the pounds keep melting away, revealing glimpses of the person I was meant to be. Confidence is growing, resilience takes hold, and a renewed sense of purpose is now guiding me forward. This isn't just about losing weight; it's about overcoming obstacles, rewriting my own story, and embracing the transformative power of divine Godly love.

Join me as I share the ups and downs of motherhood, the challenges of battling life-threatening and life-limiting illnesses, the serendipity of finding true divine godly love, and the delicate balance of nurturing a family while pursuing personal dreams. Together, we will navigate life's twists and turns, celebrating victories big and small and drawing inspiration from the profound impact that love, concern, and care can have on our life journeys.

Write a scientific book: 17 January 2023

A Scientist's Untold Feelings (A Love Story Inside the Mind): Not a scientific book

"Girl, you are a scientist. Why don't you write and publish a scientific book? You can do anything!" Guy exclaimed, displaying his characteristic ignorance, innocence, and intense confidence in me. The thought of writing a journal or book of personal experiences had never crossed my mind since I entered adulthood, but suddenly today, I am giving it serious thought and consideration. So, Guy, I am embarking on the journey of writing this book that will narrate my life story in the form of poems, short write-ups and chapters since the day I met you more than a decade ago and beyond. A sprinkling of childhood challenges is also included here and there. You have consistently been the powerful pillar of strength, hope, and unconditional love in my life; therefore, I dedicate this book to you. Knowingly or unknowingly, you were and are the catalyst that I was waiting for my entire life. Yes, Guy, you are one of the greatest miracles in my life.

I have never written a book before, but I have always nurtured a deep aspiration and desire to write and publish at least one. It feels like a childhood dream that got buried amidst the trials and tribulations of navigating life and making ends meet.

My favourite English teacher, Rita Bhatnagar Madam, always told me that I had a natural talent for English. However, I never fully believed in my own abilities. Public speaking has always been a source of fear for me, and even uttering a single line in English during my school days felt like conquering a daunting battle. Even now, as I work for a global pharmaceutical MNC, my manager provides constructive feedback that challenges me to grow. These experiences have taught me resilience, determination, and the spirit to never ever give up. I face these challenges head-on, managing this ongoing journey in both my professional and personal life.

Throughout my life, I have become accustomed to doubting my own capabilities, constantly evaluating myself, and striving for growth. This mindset has been shaped by the various rejections and life lessons I have encountered along the way.

As I pen down my thoughts and emotions, I can't help but feel a surge of excitement coursing through me.

Guy in this novel is my male version, this inner voice/inner strength/my hero that I discovered more than a decade ago and who has always redirected me to the right path. If you consider Guy as a person in my life, I leave it to your view and discretion.

I pretended I am fine!

I pretended,
I was strong and fine,
When I was told,
I can't walk ever.
When I had severe Guillain Barré Syndrome!
Although I was so behind,
I was stuck in class 8,
And all my classmates progressed to class 9!

Being the only child,
I had to smile,
To keep my parents going.

I pretended,
I was fine,
When I broke my heart,
For the first time!

I pretended,
All is well!
When not a single relationship I tried,
Worked fine!

I pretended,
I was strong and fine,
When mummy got stage 3 cancer,
Doctor gave her just 6 months' time,
And not being able to do anything for her,
Definitely felt like a crime!

I pretended,
I am strong and fine,
When I broke my ankle,
As once again, I had to be so,
Being the only child!
As my family draws strength from me,
when they see me strong and smile!

I pretended,
I am motivated and headstrong,
When I wasn't doing great career-wise,
Having great degrees but an average job,
Had certainly made me doubt my abilities!
EMIs and family responsibilities being the only child,
Had certainly brought certain wild thoughts in my mind!

I pretended,
I am positive and hopeful,
When the doctor told,
I can never be a mother!
I kept a positive attitude,
And never stopped believing,
And finally got blessed,
With a beautiful girl child!

I pretended,
I am strong and fine,
Even when I reached a weight of 100,
While it was actually killing me,
Like a silent killer!

Until I spoke candidly,
with a soul that is divine,
This soul lifted my spirits,
And left a spell undefined!
I followed everything they instructed,
With dedication and determination,
I felt a cosmic energy helping me,
Reduce this extra burden in my life!
For the first time in my life.

But alas,
Now this soul has distanced,
And I can't pretend,
That I am fine!
They are my home and family,
And how am I supposed to learn
To live without them,
When they are my lifeline!

May be with time,
I will learn,
But this time I will not be,
The same person I always used to be!
I will be distant, detached,
And will close my heart forever,
For pain is here to stay,
And only I can protect and heal this deep wound,
By not letting anyone be close to it anymore!

Chapter 2: Embracing Motherhood: A Journey of Resilience, Support, and Empowerment

In 2018, we were told by my gynaecologist that I could never be a mother due to very poor fertility as per my medical reports. The major contributing factors were PCOD, subclinical hypothyroidism, constant stressful life due to stress environment at work and very poor anti-mullerian hormone levels. I was so disheartened that I cried profoundly in the gynaecologist's office, and went back home extremely sad. My gynaecologist suggested medications followed by intrauterine inseminations. Two rounds of failed IUIs and I lost hope and a good amount of money in this. I even tried ayurvedic treatment for two months and spent another fortune which didn't work either. However, I refused to lose hope and remained extremely positive, believing that this miracle would happen one day. I always believed that I would become a mother soon and it did happen! Through dietary corrections and other measures, I conceived naturally. My pregnancy was incredibly challenging, with seven months of nausea and vomiting. Throughout this pregnancy phase, there was only one person who supported me emotionally; my mother-in-law took care of the helpless pregnant woman's needs like her own daughter. Eventually, my daughter Anvi was born on 12 February 2021, and since then, I have been learning how to navigate the joys and challenges of motherhood.

Being a mother is no easy task, especially when it comes to managing a home, cooking meals, caring for a baby, and balancing work responsibilities. Thankfully, I have been blessed with a fantastic support system at home. My mother-in-law cared for me like her own daughter during the difficult times of pregnancy, and later, my parents came to support me for several months. Even during my pregnancy, I continued working until the last week and even led two congress coverage events virtually (at work), given the circumstances of the COVID era. My experienced colleagues, who are also mothers, provided invaluable guidance and support. Guy would also motivate me, discuss my fears and concerns and hear out my heart, and share relevant posts, although they have no experience of being a woman or a mother.

The first 12 months post pregnancy, the healing phase, were extremely painful, and I struggled with weight gain and postpartum depression. However, I kept these challenges only to myself, finding comfort in the happiness my family experienced because of our little miracle. When I returned to work, I realized that my previous organization didn't offer the emotional and mental support I deserved, which led me to my current organization. I candidly expressed my desire to work while taking care of my one-year-old daughter to James, and to my surprise, he hired me without any second thoughts or judgements. Since then, it has been a true blessing. I have found balance, being able to work and raise my daughter while dedicating time to both aspects of my life.

At my current workplace, there is a strong culture of psychological safety. I feel comfortable discussing any challenges I face and working towards feasible solutions. The leadership team values every employee's voice and perspective. Experiencing such a positive and growth-oriented work culture in India, where professional and personal development go hand in hand, is truly exceptional.

Earlier this year (2023), I weighed 100 kilograms, an extremely and morbidly obese person. Thanks to my lifeline, who is like family to me, we took a deep dive into my issues and reflected on my current situation. After this, I attended a stress session by the Director of my division, which helped me identify areas of stress in my life. After this, I also attended a personal development training programme called EMERGE. During the EMERGE session, I learnt about habit formation (7 habits of highly effective people by Stephen Covey) and atomic habits (by James Clear), and immediately implemented them step by step into my daily routine. Also, thanks to my lifeline who shared countless videos on water diet and intermittent fasting and had suggested giving up sugar 100%. I heard and analysed everything in front of me and I prepared a workout and diet regimen to suit my lifestyle and something which I could commit to and make it part of my lifestyle. Guy supported me wholeheartedly in this and provided timely suggestions on what can work best. He said a very meaningful thing which stuck in my head: "If you are not passionate about your physical and mental health, make it a part of your lifestyle by incorporating it as daily habits." I got to know from the EMERGE session that it takes 21 days to form a habit and 90 days to make it a part of the lifestyle or daily routine.

As of today, on 9 June 2023, I have achieved a weight of seventy-six kilograms and have become a healthier version of myself. I am a dedicated working professional, taking care of my daughter, managing household tasks (cooking, cleaning, and looking after my husband and 90-year-old grandmother), and continuing my weight loss journey. Phase I of my weight loss journey is successfully completed, and now I am manifesting and focusing on Phase II of this journey. Phase II of my weight loss journey includes reducing 18 kilograms further, for which I need more power, dedication, and prayers! Phase III includes core strengthening and practising mindfulness and taking up a spiritual journey of happiness and exploring unexplored possibilities.

I have been able to accomplish all of this because of the unwavering support I received from my organization and because of the dedication and determination I got from my lifeline. Both of them never judged me but instead empowered me to become the best version of myself. After all, a healthy employee, both physically and mentally, is the most valuable asset an organization can have.

I am a mom, housewife, caretaker, and a full-time health care professional and I don't have domestic help!

Balancing Act: The Struggles and Triumphs of Motherhood: Newly discovered superpowers!

With a difficult oral surgery, my face was swollen, and pain filled every breath. The doctor made it clear that I couldn't take any pain medications while breastfeeding my daughter. Seeing my swollen reflection in the mirror each day reminded me of the challenges ahead as a working mother. In addition to this recovery from a very difficult oral-maxillary surgery, I am also a full-time working professional whose job needs constant undivided attention and constant stakeholder management. The weight of my responsibilities is further magnified as I am also the primary caregiver for my 89-year-old grandmother, and I have to ensure to take care of her well-being and comfort. Amidst this, juggling the demands of daily household chores, cooking meals for the family, and taking care of the needs of both my family and my little one became my new norm, and that too without any external support!

With a lot of determination and dedication, I embraced this daunting task before me and I discovered an inner strength within me, which I never knew existed. There were days when exhaustion threatened to overwhelm me, especially with the immense pain due to the oral surgery, but I persisted as

I looked at my child's face and had the desire to keep providing the best possible living environment for her.

Those painful sleepless nights and the endless responsibilities, and the physical and emotional toll were all part of this incredible journey. Those 2 months without my extended family support and juggling everything gave me a reflection of my inner strengths.

In the midst of it all, I found myself in awe of mothers everywhere across this world, human beings or animals. Whether working professionally or dedicating themselves to the full-time care of their kids and family (sacrificing so many things such as comfort, career, and beauty), their unwavering commitment is truly remarkable. It occurred to me that being a mother is not just a temporary role but is a lifelong commitment where you have to perform certain duties consistently, irrespective of how you feel, or how others make you feel.

To all the mothers out there irrespective of whether they are working or not, your sacrifices and efforts often go unnoticed, but your impact on the lives of your children can't be measured. Mothers are those unsung heroes, the steady hands of their families that shape the future generation and give their children strength and inspiration to become ideal citizens. This chapter that I have written is dedicated to all mothers—whether working or not—because being a mother itself is a feat that deserves the utmost respect and admiration.

Chapter 3: The Soulmate

What is a soulmate? Who qualifies as a soulmate, and how can they be identified? The lines from the series "Dawson's Creek" perfectly capture the essence of a soulmate:

"A soulmate is like a best friend but more. They are the one person in the world who knows you better than anyone else. They are someone who inspires you to become a better person, not by making you better, but by their mere presence. A soulmate is someone who remains with you forever. They are the one person who knew you, accepted you, and believed in you before anyone else did, even during times when no one else would. And regardless of what happens, you will always love them. Nothing can ever change that."

I have always believed that I met my soulmate in all our encounters since we met more than a decade ago. It began when we first met because of Ron and Gwen, when we visited his flat while he was searching for roommates. It continued with moments like when he apologized to me for something he did with a box of Lindt, when we played cricket together at Liverpool, during our conversations and brief interactions over the phone and in person.

I remember when he used to sleep with a thin blanket in his rented shared apartment, and I brought my duvet so that he would feel warm and not suffer from the cold. I recall his appreciation when I gifted a car and a house to my parents. I think back to when I helped him pack his belongings before his return to India. I reminisce about the times when I shared stories about my unsuccessful relationships, with Randy moderating our behaviour and not allowing him to get too close to me. I cherish our visit to Liverpool Zoo, our shared lunches at the office, the Indian Dosa lunch we had with Pixie Rose, and the time he gave me a tax return check without knowing that I needed money. All those instances where I would get upset with something he would do to make me upset/angry and he would go all stretches to patch things up with me. He constantly made me believe that I can always put all my trust in him when no one would believe in me and he will always be there to catch me when things are not going well and falling apart.

One incident that his mom narrated frequently to me was when I visited his accommodation in Delhi with my mother to invite his family to my wedding and his mother was telling me that he went out and got fish and prawns from the market and washed it and provided it to her for preparing some dishes. She mentioned that he has never done this before although she used to ask him to do so in the past. She was surprised that he did this for our visit and ended with a question, who knows what is in this boy's mind? I never talked about this incident to Guy as this would stir a different conversation. The memories continue with my stay at his parents' house in Delhi during an unsuccessful job interview, the hours-long conversations I had with his mother, and she was so curious that she would ask me often to convince her son to get married. Even funnier was when his mom called me secretively and would speak with me about him. The first time I rode his bike; when I was asking him to get married as this was his parents' wish in an auto-rickshaw which annoyed him big time; when he rescued us once again and got my better half's wedding suit at the last minute as my husband forgot to carry it from his home during our wedding; his visit to my 1 BHK flat in Pathankot Army base where I was staying with my parents; our trips to Sikkim and Arunachal Pradesh; the moments we shared during our return from Tawang; the moment I confided in him about my infertility journey at the Balaji temple; the exact moment of conception; and how my daughter was so fond of him even without meeting him. I treasure all the songs we sang together while driving, and the most significant moment was in February 2023 when he inspired me to lose weight as I was sinking and fighting obesity. All these moments now make perfect sense, why he was always there, and the memories we created together throughout our time together since we met.

What is unsaid since more than a decade

It's a build-up of more than 10 years!

Clear communication is essential in any relationship. I have always refrained from expressing my feelings since we met. However, now I believe it's better to share exactly how I've always felt instead of remaining silent. Even if you don't reciprocate these feelings, it's important for me to express them. You are like the air, omnipresent, and I love you unconditionally. You take my breath away, not only when we meet in person but at all times. No one has ever loved me as you have loved me. You have consistently been there for me, providing unwavering support. I'm not sure what this means for our future, but conveying my feelings to you feels like the right thing to do to avoid future regrets. I am already 4500 days late, and I don't wish to further delay this.

The greatest act of love is not just giving, sharing, or feeling love, but it is actually loving someone so deeply that they begin to start loving themselves. Being with you has taught me this invaluable lesson, and as I mentioned before, what you have shown me is the purest form of love that I always hoped existed. Please don't ever stop loving me. Let me reciprocate and love you even more in your life. No judgements, just genuine conversations.

I want to understand what saddens you, your fears, your heartbreaks, and your greatest triumphs. I want to hear your travel stories and more. However, I won't push you. Until then, let's explore whether our paths are destined to converge or not. You are the last person I have fallen for, and my heart is full.

My mother continues to ask me, since the day she met you, why I didn't choose you. I have also shared my feelings for you with her. Your mother and sister have asked similar questions too. Even your father inquired about this. These questions are not only challenging to answer but also burdensome to carry. You are my safe haven, always there for me, and I find solace in you (with or without your presence).

Navigating the depths of emotions

I have expressed my feelings to you, but you don't get overwhelmed or stressed about them. Personally, I dislike leaving my relationships, which are important and dear to me, in a state of confusion or uncertainty regarding my emotions. I don't expect anything in return except for the incredible bond we share, akin to Tom and Jerry!

I acknowledge that your traits, along with your reservations about relationships and your mysterious nature, are integral parts of your personality. I respect your preference for solitude and have no intention of intruding into your personal space.

These mixed feelings prompted me to be honest with you. I don't want you to get hurt in any way because of me. After more than a decade, my emotions have surfaced, despite my best efforts to keep them in check. I distance myself to protect my own feelings because I hold old-school values and have a different mindset from the norm.

However, my traits lean me towards honesty, bluntness, and loyalty to my loved ones; these are inherent traits that I sometimes find hard to control. I don't pay much attention to others' opinions of me unless they are close to me. I either go all-in or not at all.

Mind games are not my style when it comes to the people I love or in general, as it goes against my nature. However, it does hurt me when my feelings are toyed with, and I can recognize it when it happens. I'm not that naive.

Only someone like me can love in the way that I do—limitless, unconditional, and respectful of personal space. Sadly, finding this kind of love in today's world seems impossible.

Once again, if I have caused you any hurt, I sincerely apologize, as that was never my intention.

Chapter 4: Weights and Strength! The Power of True Love/Greatest Love

I gave you all the weights of my world,

And you gave me all your strength to deal with them!

The purest form of love, respect and care!

One tiny perspective on love

A woman in love can just actually be in her own little world within her brain. It is difficult to believe in today's time, but one can be as modern as possible, but when it comes to love, one can be a die-hard old school.

Being involved physically will be the last thing in her mind, but definitely not the first when she considers you as her lifeline.

An honest hardworking woman (who knows what is at stake if she takes even one wrong step) craves care, attention, and love not just in words. You need to show this in action and your behaviour. Sometimes, some men don't understand this because they don't have the brains to comprehend this very simple fact. And when such women get all these (care, attention, and love in their behaviours and action) from someone close, they consider those close relationships everything, even God.

For some rare introvert species like me, intimacy (emotional and physical) comes only when there are true feelings. And those true feelings, I have never experienced till date. Otherwise, you can be hot as a rod and yet remain untouched and ignored by weird samples like me.

Vibrations sent to the universe! The two-way street

Thoughts are like vibrations, and you can feel it when it's two-way!

And it amplifies for sure and does wonders that you never thought would have been possible otherwise.

Those innocent, fun, and cute rhymes

Girl: Matlab Kulu Manali Shimla me hone wala hai dhamal

Guy: Isilie leke jaunga acha sa rumaal

Girl: Wah tu baatein karta hai kamaal

Guy: Hope nahi Banna pade mujhe hamaal

Girl: Teri toh log denge misaal

Guy: Lagayenge misaal, Par nahi ja raha hu main Nainital

Girl: Arre ye toh tha mera agla sawal

Guy: Kahi tu ban toh nahi gaya dalal

Girl: Iski karni padegi jaach padtaal

Girl: Abhi 7 and 8 March ko tha festival of gulal

Guy: Shabash Girl

Guy: Proud of you

Guy: This was your best

Girl: Wah! When the expert says

Girl: I have reached Bangalore

Guy: Matlab Abh Bangalore ki khair nahi

Girl: Lagta hai aaj meri khair nahi

Guy: Next earthquake epicentre Bangalore

Girl: Run Guy run, warna teri khair nahi

Guy: Meri ya Anupam ki

Girl: Your title just changed from Guy to Kher, Guy Kher nahi,

Guy: Aur Guy ki skin fair bhi nahi

Girl: Cz you don't care, Teri species hai badi rare, Horses wife is called mare, Tu mere samne kara na kar zyada dare

Guy: Kya tu karegi mere saath chicken share

Girl: Warna rahegi nahi teri kher, Ye sharing k concept se me nahi hu aware

Guy: Aaj Girl on fire!

Guy: Hi yedi Girl!

Girl: Hi yeda Guy!

Guy: Tu yedi, me yeda, chal khate hai milke peda

Girl: Kya chad gaya hai tujhpe poem ka keeda

Guy: Kyunki aadmi hu main teda

Girl: Yes I agree k tu hai teda and meda!

The incomplete poem and the early morning bedtime teas!

For a girl, her first love/hero or ideal person is her father,
And as she grows up, she imagines finding someone as
caring and understanding as her father,
As she has seen how her father has treated his wife,
During good and difficult times.

Papa used to give me morning bed tea,
And then one day I got married,
Suddenly all my morning bedtime teas bid me good bye!
Then suddenly one day, they appeared,
Not by my better half,
But this person with whom I share a special bond,
Which remains undefined!
For all the days we were together,
He ensured that I get my morning bed tea,
Trust me no one has done that ever,
For me!

Precious eyes

There is something about those eyes
That can't be ignored or denied
I can look at them forever
And not get bored
Even for a second

But the moment they see me, I simply stumble and lose my mind

The last time we met
Your eyes looked different
They were deep as ocean
And had a constant twinkle
And them eyes coupled with that beautiful smile
Was a moment I captured in my mind forever and ever for myself to repeat to myself and smile

On other times
Sometimes so playful
Sometimes so restless constantly jumping from me to anything xyzee

When you look at me
I see a man with vast ocean full of love, commitment and innocence
Like my papa looks at my mumma,
Or like your papa looking at your mumma,
And when I see you looking at others
I see a naughty little person
Who is carefree and responsibility-free

Your eyes speak a thousand words
All I see is a twinkle when they see me
And it lights up my heart and soul instantly

Strange feelings!

What was this feeling today?
Did you sense something too?
Felt this connection suddenly so close,
although in different locations,
Trying to divert my mind,
I am not able to!

Reasons to live redefined

I was so fed up with life,
I had no interest to live,
Was just working like a robot,
Fulfilling everyone's demands,
Without any feelings but a default smile,

I thought this was my fate,
As life never gave me any rebate,
The only silver lining I had since we met,
My ultimate source of Vitamin P (Positivity)!
Not sure if you will believe,
But everything we spoke about,
Has always showed up in my life journey!

I had this feeling,
If I continued with my lifestyle,
I probably may not sustain beyond 40 or 39,
So, even the term insurance I took,
Has the age limit of 55,

But now,
Looks like I will have to get another term cover,
Till 75!

How I wish,
There was no COVID, and this long gap in between,
Things would have been different indeed!

I am strong enough to sustain by myself,

But even the strongest tree needs a piece of earth,

And that piece of earth my beloved, is you to me!

Don't want to be quiet no more

You held my hand
Through the darkest times
And made me believe
I can be anything I want

Devoted and dedicated
Mind, soul and body
Just to you
Since 15 May 2020
But was in love for longer time
That I always denied even to myself
And all my breathes lie
Under your sky

Slow and steady
We have nothing to hurry
So don't worry
Will always be your mate

Have stayed hidden
For a very long time
And I am sorry
For all the bad times

Transparency in relationships

Truth may hurt, but being loyal to people you really care about is the most priceless gift you can give! It may hurt them initially, but if they are really your true relationships, they will understand it!! No matter what.

Carer of your soul

You take care of all your friends,
Your family,
Like we are all part of one clan!

So who takes care of you,
When you feel alone?
Know that I am always there,
Who prays and care,
For a divine soul like you,
Who is like a diamond and so rare!

Cutting a lifeline cord?

How can you erase your existence from someone's life when they consider you as their heartbeat?

You mean they should die to erase your existence?

No beats, no life!

Let's not be angry and contribute to global warming

Kyu karta hai itna gussa,
Global warming ka mat ban tu bhi ek hissa.

Ab is gusse ki kya hai remedy,
1000 times sorry bolu ya rukna padega mujhe till I am
seventy?

Tu karta nahi ab respond,
But samajh le ye hai strong chemical bond.

Even if you throw this relation in a pond,
Mother fairy will bring it out with her wand.
Tu karte reh mujh ko abscond,
But me karti rahungi time to time respond.

You are my home and family,
And family doesn't leave by taking patli gali.

Days and weeks without a hint of you!

Without a hint of you,
My weekdays and weekends have turned into:
Monday blues,
Tedious Tuesdays,
Weeping Wednesdays,
Tiring Thursdays,
Fainted Fridays,
Sour Saturdays,
And sad Sundays!

13 years and still lost!

Stop it!
Said the mind
But this is what is keeping me going
Said the heart
And the mind lost
Once again!

Family never leaves!

Just because one apple tasted bad,
We don't stop ourselves from eating more apples!
Similarly,
One fight or misunderstanding in a meaningful relationship,
Doesn't stop you from being family!
For family always sticks around,
Through thick and thin,
And fights through difficult circumstances,
And still chooses to win!

One breath and then heartache

The breathing still continues,
Life still continues,
For I have to play my part,
Although the pain in heart stings like a dart!

I can conceal,
With a big smile,
For life has taught,
All these lessons,
And I will live like there is no tomorrow,
And a life without any regrets!

Because my feelings are pure,
And thus, this heartache has no cure!

Chapter 5: Overcoming Challenges: Showing Up Even at the Lowest Times

Severe Guillain Barré Syndrome (GBS) in school where I was told I can't walk ever again, may never conceive, one-sided love and rejection, meaningless boyfriends who were only after one thing rather than having a meaningful relationship, stage III signet ring cell carcinoma of Ma, Papa's low income, education loan, my complex open bimalleolar ankle fracture, infertility, severe obesity, financial pressure, and the list continues.

Even worse, not having anyone to talk about all this. No siblings and temporary school friends due to Papa's transferable defence job that made me study in so many different places in India. A confused, scared little girl who was trying so hard to make her own identity. As I grew up, I was a lonely soul looking for a place to call my home!

Icing on top, the male predators constantly trying to get something. I can never forget that bus conductor who would touch intentionally on the chest and back, no matter how hard I tried to protect myself, every time, I would try to board and leave the school bus. And he did this to several girls, but we were so scared of him that we never told anyone and would try out ways to avoid him touching us. For example, putting a sweater on the back, and covering the front with both arms, tiffin boxes, and books. And the worse part was, we were not even aware of whom to tell these things because everyone would think that we were responsible for this. Which 5th/6th standard girl would like to be touched like that? This is not where it ends! So, I preferred walking 4–5 kilometres or taking my bicycle whenever possible, instead of being a victim every single day. In a city like Agra, with extreme weather conditions, attending school every day whether it was hot, cold, or rainy, didn't matter. Showing up mattered!

When I was admitted as a paralysed patient due to severe GBS to the ICU of the army hospital in New Delhi, one sweeper touched my chest when he saw total isolation. The fan was on and the cloth on top of me had flown off, and this person instead of covering my body, touched me. I was just 13 years old. I still remember seeing patients from the Kargil War in R&R Hospital, New Delhi. Since I was in the ICU, I would only see the most difficult cases and survivors of the devastating war! But, about that time, Kaho Na Pyaar Hai was released and the songs from this movie acted like a saviour for me. Watching Hrithik Roshan and Amisha Patel dance to the song "Dil mera, har baar ye…" was pure bliss!

Then another incident was in class 9th after my recovery from GBS. We were travelling to Assam on a night service bus. I was sitting next to the window and my mother was sitting next to me. I love travelling since childhood, so although it was late at night, I was looking outside the window and pretending to sleep at the same time. Then suddenly, I felt a hand on my thighs and he opened the zipper of my jeans. Thankfully, it was December and I was wearing 4–5 layers inside my jeans. I immediately became conscious and told my mother what just happened. Now, even she was scared of this incident, so she politely asked that person to straighten his seat. We switched our seats, Mom sat near the window and I sat next to the aisle, blocking his view of me. She also indirectly communicated to him that she is aware of what he has done and would complain to the driver if that doesn't stop. Phew! What a relief this was. Having my mom beside me and protecting me like a hero!!

Even worse is when family members try to molest you. On the same trip, one of my uncles would try to grab me so tight and try to rub his face all over my body, and I would just shout out loud and try to get out of his grip and run to a family member and complain about him. Meeting him was a nightmare and I don't have any good feelings about that monster uncle. But looking at the brighter side, my mother always taught me to shout out loud if I felt things were unsafe, and that is what exactly I did. Shouting out loud would make him nervous and release me, and I would run as fast as I could!

Throughout these challenging phases of life (especially being a single girl child), there was one thing I never stopped doing and was consistent about: getting up, dressing up, and showing up with a big smile, no matter what the situation was like.

However, throughout my life journey, I was actually looking for a miracle to happen to save me from this vicious cycle and intense pain I had gone through in my life. Had I continued living the way I was living till January 2023, I would have died in the next 2–3 years due to a heart attack or something.

I was raised believing that I am responsible for my family and I have to fulfil duties such as getting my parents their dream home, car and financial needs, and their health. Then after marriage, this only amplified as I was looking after two families: my parents and in-laws. It further increased when I had my daughter and my financial burden only increased.

Someone has written very aptly:

Some of us are building from scratch: No inheritance, no connections, no backups.

Just blood, sweat, and skills.

Persistence and consistency!

14 May 2010: Thoughts on memorable moments

Yesterday somebody asked me about a memorable moment of life. I told the day when I came out of ICU alive after an ordeal of 45 days (on a ventilator) and saw birds flying against the bright blue sky!!

When a poem reads you!

Often,
You read a poem.
While at other times,
It's the poem that reads you,
And defines your situation!

Gratitude thought and tweet

Practising gratitude does help in keeping negativity at bay and managing difficult days with a positive mindful attitude/ outlook.

Maja Howard: Meaningful progress happens when your actions align with the vision you have set for yourself.

Bitu: To perform those actions for meaningful progress, a clear process should also be present and that should be clearly written down because without a process, consistency, and dedication a vision may blur and become meaningless in the long run!

Weird intuitions! First childhood love

I used to write poems in high school; around forty of them were dedicated to a person I was totally into. I compiled it into a book and gave it to him. Unfortunately, he rejected me and returned the book. After this heart-breaking incident, I stopped writing altogether.

In my graduation days, I had a classmate named XXX who had a striking resemblance to me and people would often confuse between the two of us. They would address me as XXX and her as Girl!

Then, on July 1, 2020, out of nowhere, this person called me. When I asked him about his marriage plans, he revealed that he was planning to get married. For this, can you guess what my response was? I said, "So, you're getting married to XXX?" This guy was completely startled by my response, and he dropped his phone on the floor and the call got disconnected. He called me back a second time and asked who told me about this as no one was aware of it. It just came out spontaneously from my mouth without any stalking, previous knowledge, or being in touch with any of his or my school friends.

How did that name come out of my mouth then?

Just pure strong intuitions! I still wonder, but I have made peace with this episode.

Dreams and goals so powerful!

There are possibilities,
That
I am more than what I think of me!

I am amazed,
How I have started transforming myself,
To a better me, a healthier me,
Although the journey is,
Only half-way through!

Some days are tough,
But you need to learn,
To hold your own hand,
Catch yourself up and keep going!

The only person, who can really inspire you,
Is the quiet little dream,
That you conceived,
As a child and forgotten about it!

Some are lucky, to be privileged,
While some are not,
And their paths are made,
Through arid lands, disappointments and draught!

So next time you fail/fall/get rejected,
Remember that a better future is being redirected,
And changing courses can be painful,
But those you keep going, no matter what the situation is,
Win and inspire others to dive deep within!

For some colleagues, goodbyes are never forever!

Thank you for being the beacon of hope,

A true guide who always inspired me to be the best I can be!

And I did know that with your guidance,

I will always succeed!

Your openness and continuous warm support,

Both at the same time,

Have helped me gain knowledge in neurology and immunology,

Molecule 1 and Molecule 2,

To be more specific!

You have done a fantastic job,

As a Publication Lead.

Now I am just thinking,

How awesome you would be,

In the next organization you join!

I am grateful for everything!

And let's stay in touch forever,

For Medical Affairs is global but so niche.

We may cross paths again,

And it would be awesome to work,

With someone as amazing as you always have been!

Be the frog and leap again

Take a leap of faith,
And breathe again.
What is beyond those fears,
Just a little harder work and pain.

But just keep reminding yourself,
That after every dusk,
A stormy night,
The hidden sun will shine again!

My bestie and Girl

North and south,
When I am in Bangalore,
She is sitting in Delhi,

School is the time,
Since we know each other,
We have met only once or twice,
Since we completed our bachelor's!

Still this distance,
Didn't dilute our feelings,
And love and care,
For each other!

We sense each other in pain,
And our connection regains!
Every time we sense,
Either one of us is in need or danger!

When you know,
Such connections are rare!
You keep them watering, and keep them alive,
And tend to forgive, all the mistakes!

For having deep connections,
Even when you don't meet,
Is meaningful and rare!

For love is happiness!

One thing that you need to remember,
Life goes on,
Yes, it continues!
With or without,
Yours truly and forever!

You are your only cover,
And you need to learn to be on your own,
In the backseat of your rover,
As you age, you getting older,
These cloudy thoughts get over!

But do make memories,
Lots of them!
Never stop loving,
For love is happiness!

And you need to pick whatever is left,
And make your own beautiful story cover!

Moon and Venus

I am very fond of the moon,
Even fonder of the beautiful relationship,
that the moon and Venus display over time in the sky!

One day they are closest to each other,
Other days they are away from each other!

And some days,
the moon is not even there!

But Venus waits patiently,
shining all alone,
Until the moon arrives all over again!

She will always be around you!

This will be the first Mother's Day when Auntie is not physically present amongst us, and we remember the pure soul of Auntie who loved and cared for you, us, and your family with all her heart. Her dedication to your well-being was unwavering, and her love knew no bounds. Auntie's selflessness and nurturing spirit were a testament to the power of a mother's love.

In this world that can often feel harsh and unforgiving, Auntie's love provided a haven of warmth and safety to you, a nest which was cosy and protective. Her memory serves as a reminder that the most important things in life are the love and connections we share and cherish with loved and close ones.

So, on this Mother's Day, let us honour the memory of Auntie and all the loving mothers who have passed on before us. Their legacy lives on in the love they have given, and the memories they have left behind.

And I lost once again!

You were playing a game
Now you are stuck well in my heart and brain
I feel it's going to rain
That is all the heart pain
What did you gain?

The touch of your hand
The moments filled with fun and happiness
Mini rhymes
And rounds of chai
Travel plans and destinations
Being there every time I was my weakest

Mixed messages all the time

Virtual and real

Was it all part of a plan
Is this how you find out!
How I feel?

Fears and demons all faded away! (poem written with chatgpt)

Sharing my biggest fears and facing them with your guidance was very liberating. I am not worried or scared of those anymore. I can face my demons without any fears, I guess. It just took me half of my life to understand this. You already are on the upper hand because this is not a struggle for you at all. I think soon I will be unstoppable now.

Beneath the veil of my deepest fears,
I stood alone, with unsaid trembling tears.
But then, I found a hand to hold,
And with your guidance, I grew so bold.

I shared my heart and my pains,
And slowly and steadily, I have shed all my chains.
The grip of fear is no longer strong,
I have faced my demons, and now they were gone.

It took me half a life to understand,
The power of this freeing hand.
You stood beside me, strong and sure,
With patience, kindness, and a sure-shot cure.

Though you may have an upper hand,
And you have faced your fears in different lands,
Our journeys are unique, you see,
Yet, together, we find liberty.

I think soon, I'll be unstoppable,
My spirit so bright and so full.
For facing my insecurities and fears with you have shown,
That I can learn, grow and stand alone.

So let us journey on, oh my dear,
And share the courage that we can lend to each other.
For in this life, we all must face,

Our demons with a steadfast grace.

Scientific poem 1: Lupus and multiple sclerosis make me feel all right

When I write,
I feel all right,
whether it's day or night,
Lupus and Multiple sclerosis,
you are my energy source like ketosis,
slow and steady,
but sure and ample,
You inspire me like a candle,
for I know that when I write,
I feel all right!

The poem I wrote after 18 long years got me the best poetry award in my organization! I wrote this poem because I found my ikigai during all our conversations and interactions. When someone influences you to this level that you only become a better version of yourself with each passing day for more than a decade, you know that you have found your greatest strength and the truest form of love!

Scientific poem 2: Global Medical Affairs and my life as a Guillain Barré Syndrome survivor

When I was in school,
my life wasn't cool,
Alas, I was diagnosed with Guillain Barré Syndrome,
and I was told I can't walk,
that Indian Air Force physiotherapist,
was definitely not a therapist,
heck, I churned those words,
and showed everyone, I can walk!

As a patient, my family was given an information leaflet,
little did I know,
that when I will grow,
I will end up in a relationship with those,
severe GBS happened in 1998,
and now is 2023,
I am penning down my thoughts in a poem!

That information leaflet gave my family so much information,
and I learnt how to write with a pen,
eat with a spoon,
walk on feet and run on toes,
and master those fine motor skills!

Global Medical Communications,
to doctors and patients,
yes, I proudly tell!

that I am here because I went through hell,
and came out well.

Life is too short to be serious all the time,
tough times come,
but that's all right, with all that pain,
it's experience that we gain,
and we learn to dance in rain!

To all the healthcare professionals and Global Medical
Affairs personnel,
it's because of the hard work you do,
patients with little or no hope,
recover, and they learn in life to spread a ray of hope learnt
during those tough times!

Diya: Encounter with a soul passenger

While returning from Guwahati airport to Bangalore, I had the pleasure of meeting a young girl named Diya from Kerala. She appeared nervous and lost, unsure of what to do or where to go as we stood near the security check area. Without hesitation, I approached her and inquired if it was her first time travelling from an airport. Tentatively, she confirmed it and asked for guidance on the next steps. I willingly offered my assistance, walking her through the security check process and explaining everything she needed to know. Throughout our interaction, she remained lost in her own deep thoughts.

I noticed that Diya had an iPhone with a poor battery life, constantly charging it to keep it running. Curiosity led me to ask her about her feelings regarding her first air travel experience. She expressed a mix of excitement and fear. Diya mentioned that she is a B.Com graduate working at Decathlon in Kerala and had come to Bangalore for a two-day training session at Bangalore Decathlon. However, she had no place to stay and was unfamiliar with the area. Taking charge, I opened my Make My Trip app and searched for pocket-friendly yet decent hotels near her destination. It was apparent that she depended on me to find a safe place for her, and with her phone battery depleted once again, I took the initiative to book the hotel using my own phone, even making the necessary calls to arrange the hotel.

As we waited for our Uber cab, Diya shared stories of her recent travels. She excitedly recounted her road trip to Meghalaya with some friends, emphasizing her passion for the journey itself rather than the destination. She spoke animatedly for a good seven minutes, and I found myself captivated by her narrative, choosing not to interrupt. By the time she finished her tale, our Uber had arrived, signalling the end of our time together. We bid farewell, and the encounter left such a unique and refreshing impression on me that I felt compelled to document it.

Diya, with her pure-hearted innocence and burgeoning sense of adventure, had just embarked on her journey through life.

Thoughts from 10 April 2023:
Poem dedicated to my human Guy

This poem is for you,

you guide me to be a healthier me,

You're my beacon of hope, a friend indeed,

You inspire me to be the best I can be,

And I know that with you, I'll succeed.

You see my potential where I see only flaws,

And encourage me to keep going,

You always pick me up when I fall (not just this),

And remind me of the progress that's showing.

With your guidance and support,

I'm shedding the weight that held me down,

And as I've grown stronger, I've learnt to report,

On the blessings that are all around.

You remind me to take care of myself,

To nourish my body and my soul,

And as I find my way to better health,

I know that I am never alone.

You never judged or criticized (although ye baat puri tarah

sach nahi),

But always offered a helping hand,

And with you by my side,

I knew I could make a stand.

So now I want to say thank you,

For being my lifeline and my guide,

And know that I'll always be there too,

Whenever you need me by your side.

Together we can conquer anything,

And achieve our dreams and more,

For you inspire me every day,

To be the best that I can be and more.

2 March 2022: Grateful. My mother is a cancer survivor. 9 years cancer-free. Kicking cancer butt.

I started this blog at a time when my mom was diagnosed with cancer (2014) and I had no one to share my thoughts with (since I am a single child with super strict and conservative parents, where even uttering the word boyfriend would give good thrashes from my mother). I am timid in nature, so I didn't dare to write as much as I would have liked to write and post. But I still managed to write a few posts and add them here on WordPress.

Now that I am revisiting this blog after so many years, I feel so proud to have been able to overcome all those fears and doubts and conquer all those challenges.

My mom, my lifeline, who was diagnosed with stage 3 signet ring cell carcinoma of the stomach and was given a deadline of no more than 6 months back in 2014, celebrated my daughter's first birthday.

Now conceiving and having my own baby is another series of blogs altogether, but in this blog, I specifically want to thank that superior power who made all this possible.

From having the dilemma of my mother's survival from cancer 9 years ago to creating memories for life with my mother and daughter, I am so proud to say that I have come a long way: from nothing to a super successful journey of preserving life and celebrating it every single second.

2 March 2023: My weaning story

For the past few days, I was trying to wean off my 1-year-old baby girl. And yet she was persistent on taking my milk. So today (2nd March 2022), at 3 am when she was crying to have my milk, I allowed her to have my milk but I started a conversation saying that she is a big girl and it is now high time for her to leave mumma's milk. She is a grown-up child now and eats soup, rice, and dal and drinks apple juice, she should leave mumma's milk as everyone will tease her. I had a deep conversation with her about this for nearly 15 minutes.

To my surprise, she sat down and listened carefully to everything I said. After this, she hugged my breast and held it for some time. And then I offered her a bottle with some leftover milk; she drank that and slept.

I was shocked at how a tiny 1-year-old baby listened to her mom and just soothed herself and slept away. I wrote this at 3.45 am… I am so proud of my little baby girl who understood something from the deep conversation we had at night!

So… When the going gets tough, the tough get going

A red Alto driver, who was driving weirdly, caught my attention while driving back home. I decided to move ahead and keep a safe distance from that vehicle as the driver was driving weirdly and it looked quite unsafe. I managed to take over that car and felt like a winner because I got a feeling that I am saved from a bad omen. But then suddenly, a flock of sheep blocked the road and created a traffic jam within no time. There was a silver Duster just in front of me, and I was literally waiting for the car to move ahead in the traffic. I was a confident driver who could handle any road situation in a city like Pune until this happened. I was returning from the market with my mother, a soon bride-to-be who went out for jewellery shopping with her mother on a fine lazy Sunday afternoon when most of the suburban defence population of Pune sits back at home and enjoys family time.

Suddenly, I felt as if someone has hit me from behind. I lost control and fell on the right-hand side of the road. My mother jumped like a TV actor and stood behind. I was recovering from the fall and then suddenly, alas! I heard the sound of 'breaking ice cubes'. It took me a second to realize that the car has ran over my foot and I have broken my ankle. I started shouting "Holy fuck! Holy shit! What the fuck just happened. How will I go to work! My entire career is at stake." I panicked and started looking for my lost foot in the road as I was unable to feel my foot as a part of my body. When I saw that my foot is attached to my body, I tried to stand but my broken foot was doing a break dance like Michael Jackson. That was an immensely painful moment but I managed to get a funny feeling during that instance. I shouted at the Alto driver and all I could see was my blood splattered around. My mother was in a state of shock to see me in pain and smeared with blood. The car driver came out and picked me up and assisted me to sit in his defective car. I swore at him like anything and told him to take me to the Indian Air Force Hospital (sick quarters) nearby. I picked my branded Clark flip flops as I knew they are really expensive and in the meantime, someone parked my Scooty on the side of the road. I shouted at that person and asked him to hand over my bike keys as the bike belonged to me. The guy with my bike keys was not handing over the keys and I growled again and at swore him to hand over my bike keys! I shouted: "You damn fucker, give me those bike keys, that bike is mine. The guy with my bike keys stumbled and gave me the keys immediately!" I then instructed the guilty driver to take me to the medical centre and directed him to the destination.

8 August 2015: Celebrating lights of cancer survival

A year and a half of cancer survival combated with great bravery and inspiration to so many others: Lots of respect to my warrior. My mother

Keep cancer on the top of your head and it will eat you completely; place it below your feet and kick it… you will enjoy the game.

10 July 2014: State of mind – cancer diaries

Sleepless and nervous, not because of a fabulous happening moment in my life but for the first round of chemotherapy that mom will be going through tomorrow! There is so much dilemma and confusion about what is the fate of my life… my mother's life. Is it going to work or…??

There are so many questions in my mind right now. Even though there is so much information available on the internet, nothing is clear! I had imagined my life to be happy with Ash, his family, and my mom and dad but alas! What has happened? Things are falling apart.

For the first time in my life, I want to be rich, super rich and treat my mum with the best treatment options available! I wish I had discovered or invented some way of curing signet carcinoma of the stomach for my mom! There was a time when I wanted to discover a treatment for the disease I suffered from, the G B Syndrome. Now this stupid stomach cancer of my mom.

Does God really exist? He has given only big problems in my family's lives, but we have always fought bravely in all situations and overcome them. But this stupid cancer is so different! We know the exact reason why things can change in future. My mom is my best friend. She is my life and the heart of my small nuclear family. I have lived my life to make my parents proud of me and my achievements. My mom and dad are the sole reasons I have worked so hard my entire life.

I fought back against GBS and lived the life they wanted me to live.

A normal life without any disabilities. I am nervous, I am sleepless, I am worried! Thinking of ways to stop Mum from going far away from me. Food, lifestyle, being super rich, being superstitious. What? What can stop me from losing her or seeing her in pain? My mind is so numb now that I feel stuck.

29 June 2014: The daily battle in my life

The biopsy reports revealed Signet Ring Cell Carcinoma. Mum was with me when I was collecting the reports from the pathology lab. I had tears rolling down my cheeks and the entire world around me stopped for a while. It took me a while to realize that my mother has been diagnosed with cancer! Why me! My mother! The person I love the most in this entire world was diagnosed with this dreadful disease. I had thousands of questions in my mind, and a very painful heart and even Dad or Ash were not there to share this situation of our life. I turned my face away and tried to control myself and my mum was asking me, "Is everything ok? Are the reports normal?" I controlled the tone of my voice and replied, "Pretty much. Nothing much to worry." She kept asking me the entire way to the doctor's clinic if everything is fine or if something serious has been detected. I told her one thing, 'I will not let anything happen to you. It is my promise. The report says you are facing a condition but this condition is treatable.' She asked the receptionist in the Gastroenterological clinic if everything is ok with her reports. I indicated the receptionist with my eyes not to tell her anything. The receptionist told Mum that the doctor will tell her what treatments will be needed to be done and everything is fine. We were waiting for our turn to meet the specialist, and when our turn came, I went inside with my mum and out of nowhere tears started rolling down my eyes continuously. Mum was busy talking to the doctor and so she did not see my tears but the specialist saw me breaking down.

He was kind to me and assured me that they will try their best to treat my mother. My mother was like, tell me sir what is wrong with me? He said this is cancer. And he was worried this might come up in the biopsy.

I was broken from the inside, but I told myself that I have to stay strong in front of everyone. We returned home. Dad came to pick us up from the bus station and Mum told him in a one-liner:

"Honey, I have stomach cancer!" Dad was stunned for a while. He had just returned from work and suddenly this news! I told him let's reach home and then will let you know about the reports. Dad was like OK. We reached home, and on the way, none of us dared to speak a single word to anyone. Complete silence. We decided not to tell Grandma anything about her condition as she will be very upset and might get unwell because of this.

It's a daily battle that I am living with since. I am seeing my mum fight this disease.

Thoughts from my diary: 1 January 2005 (Getting old)

Life has become empty and there is nothing to explain about it. Life has so much meaning but still, sometimes it means nothing. The body or the soul feels hollow whenever the mind searches for the God within itself. Every time a sound whose resonance is like the cymbal hits the mind and again vanishes, this shaken mind becomes very lonesome. During this moment, everything becomes dark and nothing is clear. The mind remains in a state of dilemma. A dilemma of this crux life. When the silver covering of the jewel when gets removed, it becomes ugly and is of no use as no one likes worn-out things. But what about this life? When one transfers to an old, dusky person, does the worth of his life decrease? If not, does it remains the same? If it remains the same, then why are they not embraced as a part of this society, and why are they neglected as if they are a burden on our society? Life is precious. Yes, because we are still existing and there are still generations that have to exist. We trust the lord and pray to him coz he gave us this life and made us able to be such. We have a soul within us which is immortal and is above every truth of this universe. I can see, feel, and converse with thee coz I am alive.

A DAY

A day from this life has gone,

flew like a birdie from the nest.

Away is the destiny to lord,

Let's search and hope that we will get it.

Soul is immortal, and so am 'I',

Even if I'll be dead, but not the 'I'.

Words will be vanished, everything will destroy,

But the new is waiting, to be described.

Virginity of the lives has gone,

But it can be redefined.

Flashes of wind struggle and withdraw,

but the broadness of 'it' never ends.

8 June 2014: Thoughts from my diary on New Year's Day, 2014

Another year, another month, another day, and yet another moment! Today is the first day of 2014. 2013 was a mixed year of loads of failures and a few successes. However, I started this new year's moment with a beautiful firework with Ritu in Manchester Piccadilly Gardens. The twinkling lights reaching the heights of the Manchester wheel were magically beautiful. The cold breeze with the warmth of the sparkling lighting was mesmerizing.

It was 11 pm. Cold wet night on the 31st of the last month of the year. I still cannot forget that when I came out of the house, it was raining heavily. Ritu and I were in doubt about going to the city centre just to see the damp fireworks. In doubt and confusion, we both stepped out of our houses and started our journey towards Piccadilly Gardens. I stood for 32 minutes waiting for the bus to come and no buses showed up. There were hundreds of buses coming from Piccadilly Gardens towards Rusholme but not a single bus towards the gardens. It was frustrating because Ritu had already reached the gardens and she was waiting for me in the cold. At 11.22 pm, I started walking after I realized that it was going to be a busy night. I reached near the Stopford Building of Manchester University and a fully loaded bus started approaching the next bus stop. I ran like a wild rat running after a piece of cheese but still managed to miss the bus. It was 11.40 and I was still near the Red Chilli restaurant. I was having a mixed feeling that

I might miss the fireworks in Piccadilly. I started walking very fast and then just another bus just passed by. I missed four buses like this. The fifth bus did not stop at the bus stop I was waiting at but stopped at the previous and the next bus stop! I had a huge adrenaline rush because the more I was trying to get a bus and make up my time, the harder it was becoming. Finally, at 11.45 PM, the sixth bus came miraculously out of nowhere and stopped at the bus stop. The bus driver seemed to be an angel sent from heaven for me. I wanted to hug the bus driver for being so good and generous towards me. I reached Piccadilly Gardens at 11.55 and ran towards Ritu, who was standing next to the KRO bar. We crawled across the crowd for a brilliant view of the fireworks for 10 minutes. I always remember Tinker Bell and the pixie dust when I see fireworks. It is a magical experience!! I went to Geeta Bhavan temple with Anil, Arvind and two other common friends in Anil's car. I was remembering the last new year which was cold and miserable. But this new year's day outscored my bad experiences of last year and this is what is important. Being optimistic, more confident and happier.

Piccadilly Gardens, Manchester M1 1RG, UK

Chapter 6: The Conclusion: Unfolding Life's Canvas

In today's fast-paced world, where relationships often seem fragile and disposable, it is reassuring to witness the strength of bonds within our own country. We live in a society that cherishes and values the importance of family and stands by one another through thick and thin. It is a testament to our collective belief that true relations are worth fighting for, even when faced with challenges and conflicts.

While blood ties may hold a special place in our hearts, we have come to realize that the strength of a relationship is not solely determined by genetics. True connections can be forged through shared experiences, mutual understanding, and constant support. These bonds, built on trust and love, transcend the limitations of blood and can be just as profound and meaningful.

In a world where it is easy to walk away and seek peace in separation, we choose to stand together. We recognize that relationships require effort, compromise, and a willingness to overcome obstacles. We understand that the true value of a relationship lies in its ability to weather storms and emerge stronger on the other side.

Our country, with its rich tapestry of cultures, traditions, and diverse communities, exemplifies the power of enduring relationships. It is in the warmth of our extended families, the loyalty of our friends-turned-family, and the support of our communities that we find solace and strength. We celebrate the bonds that have been nurtured over time, bonds that transcend the limitations of bloodlines and extend into the depths of our hearts.

Let us remember that relationships worth fighting for are the ones that enrich our lives and shape our identities. They remind us of our shared humanity and the inherent need for connection. By embracing the power of these non-blood relationships, we embrace a broader definition of family, one that extends beyond genetics and embraces the essence of love, understanding, and constant support.

In a world that often emphasizes the temporary and uncertain, let us hold dear those relationships that endure. Let us treasure the connections that defy conventional boundaries and find solace in knowing that true relationships can thrive without blood ties. It is through these bonds, strengthened by love, commitment, and resilience, that we weave a tapestry of relationships that enrich our lives and define our collective spirit.

So, let us continue to stand for each other, to fight for the relationships that bring us joy and fulfilment. And may our country always serve as a beacon of hope, reminding us that true connections are worth preserving, nurturing, and celebrating.

As I conclude this book, I am filled with a profound sense of gratitude and awe for the journey that life has taken me on till date. It has been a tapestry woven with threads of joy, pain, love, resilience, and growth. Through the narratives, poems, and chapters that I have shared, I have laid bare the intricacies of my experiences as a mother, a caregiver, a survivor, and a seeker of peace and inner strength.

Each chapter of my life has unfolded with its own unique challenges and triumphs. From the moment I held my child in my arms and embarked on the path of motherhood, I realized that it would be a journey of self-discovery and transformation. The balance between work and family, the trials of infertility and disease, and the unrelenting support for my mother through her battle with cancer – these chapters have shaped me into the person I am today.

In the midst of it all, I found comfort and inspiration in the power of words. Through poetry, I gave voice to my deepest emotions and desires. Each verse captured a fragment of my soul, allowing me to navigate the complexities of life with clarity and resilience. Whether it was the longing for a child, the celebration of love, or the mourning of loss, the poems became a sanctuary where my thoughts and feelings found refuge. This inner voice in the form of poems was lost a long time back due to a major heartbreak which I never thought I can recover from. But, today, I know that true care and feelings and having this gift of writing can heal me and may help others find strength for their life journeys.

The story of my infertility journey taught me the true meaning of perseverance. It was a chapter filled with uncertainty and heartache, but it also revealed the strength of the human spirit. The support of my loved ones, my lifeline, and the unwavering belief in the possibility of life's miracles carried me through the darkest moments. And when I finally held my child in my arms, I knew that every tear shed and every setback faced was worth it.

The encounter with Guillain Barré Syndrome was a chapter of immense challenge and resilience. It tested my physical and mental fortitude, pushing me to the brink of my capabilities. But in that struggle, I discovered the depths of my inner strength and the power of determination. It was a reminder that we are capable of overcoming even the most daunting obstacles when we have faith in ourselves and the support of those who love us.

The narrative of my mother's cancer survival was an embodiment of the indomitable human spirit. It showcased the beauty of courage and resilience in the face of adversity. Witnessing her battle, I was reminded of the fragility and preciousness of life. It compelled me to cherish every moment, to be present with my loved ones, and to live this fragile life with purpose and gratitude.

Through it all, I juggled the demands of work, family, and caregiving. The weight of responsibilities seemed insurmountable at times, but I found strength in knowing that I was not alone. The support and love of my family and lifeline, the unwavering presence of my extended family, and the camaraderie of fellow mothers all became pillars of support, holding me steady in life's journey.

As I reflect on my journey, I am struck by the universality of motherhood. It transcends borders, cultures, and species. It is a role that demands undivided commitment and selflessness. Whether working outside the home or dedicating oneself to the care of family, mothers are the unsung heroes who shape the future generation.

To all the mothers out there, your sacrifices and efforts may often go unnoticed, but the impact you have on the lives of your children is immeasurable. Your love, dedication, and resilience are the foundation upon which their dreams are built. The world may not always acknowledge the depth of your contributions, but the legacy you leave behind is eternal.

In closing, I want to express my deepest gratitude to all those who have been a part of my journey – my lifeline and my family.

www.ingramcontent.com/pod-product-compliance
Lightning Source LLC
Chambersburg PA
CBHW032022140726
47988CB00017BA/1126